Real Science-

Pre-Level I

Laboratory Workbook

Rebecca W. Keller, Ph.D.

Illustrations: Janet Moneymaker and Rebecca Keller

Real Science-4-Kids: Physics Pre-Level I Laboratory Workbook

ISBN 978-0-9823163-2-0

Published by Gravitas Publications, Inc.
4116 Jackie Road SE, Suite 01
Rio Rancho, NM 87124

Printed in United States

Gravitas
Publications Inc.

A note from the author

Hi! In this curriculum you are going to learn the first step of the scientific method:

Making good observations!

In Physics making good observations is very important. Each experiment in this workbook has different sections. There is a section called "Observe it" where you will make observations. There is a section called "Think about it" where you will answer questions. There is a section called "Test it" where you set up an experiment to observe. There is a section called "What did you discover?" where you will write down or draw what you observed in the experiment. And finally, there is a section called "Why?" where you will learn about why you may have observed certain things.

These experiments will help you learn the first step of the scientific method and... they're lots of fun!

Enjoy!
Rebecca W. Keller, Ph.D.

Contents

Experiment 1

Falling Objects

I. Observe it

❶ Take two tennis balls and hold them at chest level with your arms pointing straight.

❷ Release the two objects from your hands at the same time.

❸ Watch carefully to see how they land.

❹ Record what you see using words or pictures.

❺ Repeat steps ❶-❹ using different objects such as:

> ❖ an orange and an apple
>
> ❖ a tennis ball and a rubber ball
>
> ❖ an apple and a tennis ball
>
> ❖ a rubber ball and an apple
>
> ❖ an orange and a tennis ball

Object 1   Object 2

_____   _____

Object 1

Object 2

_____

_____

Object 1   Object 2

_____   _____

Object 1   Object 2

_____   _____

Object 1

_____

Object 2

_____

Object 1   Object 2

_____   _____

Object 1   Object 2

_____   _____

II. Think about it

❶ Are the objects falling at the same time? How can you tell?

_____

_____

_____

❷ Are there any changes you would make to your experiment? Holding the objects higher? Holding the objects lower?

_____

_____

_____

❸ Repeat the experiment for one set of objects using one change you thought about.

❹ Record your observations on the next page.

Object 1

Object 2

_____

_____

III. What did you discover?

1. Was it easy or difficult to relase the objects at the same time? Why or why not?

_____

_____

_____

2. Was it easy or difficult to observe the falling? Why or why not?

_____

_____

_____

3. Did all of the objects land at the same time? Why or why not?

_____

_____

_____

4. Did the changes you chose to make to your experiment help? Why or why not?

_____

_____

IV. Why?

Galileo Galilei discovered that when he let two objects of different weights fall from the same height, they always landed at the same time. This seems opposite to what you might think would happen. It seems like a heavier object would fall faster than a lighter object. But this is not what happens. Your observations showed that two objects of different weights will hit the ground at the same time. Why?

Things fall because of gravity. Gravity is a force that makes the objects on the earth stay on the earth. You will learn about forces in Chapter 2. Gravity pulls everything down towards the center of the earth. When you hold two objects in your hands, gravity is pulling on them. Every object has gravity pulling on it all the time. Gravity pulls on apples in the same way that it pulls on tennis balls. Gravity pulls on oranges in the same way that it pulls on rubber balls. Everything has the same force of gravity pulling on it at the same time. So, an apple (that is heavier than a tennis ball) has the same amount of gravity pulling on it as the tennis ball. Both the tennis ball and the apple start off with exactly the same amount of gravity pulling on them at the same time, and the amount of gravity pulling on them never changes.

Once the objects are released, they fall at the same speed because they have the same amount of gravity pulling on them at the same time. It doesn't matter how heavy they are. That is what Galileo and YOU discovered by doing this experiment.

V. Just for fun

What do you think would happen if you dropped an orange and a cotton ball or feather at the same time?

Try it.

Record your observations.

Orange   Cotton ball
                                (or feather)

Experiment 2

Get To Work!

I. Observe it

❶ Take a marshmallow and observe its color, shape, and size. Write or draw your observations in the space under "Before" on the next page.

❷ Take the marshmallow and place it in the center of your palm.

❸ Close your hand around the marshmallow and squeeze it with your palm and fingers.

❹ Observe your effort—muscles, hands, and fingers.

❺ Observe the marshmallow after you have squeezed it. Write or draw your observations in the space under "After."

❻ Repeat steps ❶-❺ with several other objects such as:

- ❖ rubber ball
- ❖ tennis ball
- ❖ lemon or lime
- ❖ rock
- ❖ banana

Marshmallow

Before

_____

_____

_____

_____

After

_____

_____

_____

_____

Before

_____

_____

_____

_____

_____

After

_____

_____

_____

_____

_____

Before

_____

_____

_____

_____

```
┌─────────────────────────────────────────────┐
│                                               │
│                                               │
│                                               │
│                                               │
│                                               │
│                                               │
└─────────────────────────────────────────────┘
```

After

_____

_____

_____

_____

```
┌─────────────────────────────────────────────┐
│                                               │
│                                               │
│                                               │
│                                               │
│                                               │
└─────────────────────────────────────────────┘
```

Before

_____

_____

_____

_____

_____

After

_____

_____

_____

_____

Before _____

_____

_____

_____

_____

After

_____

_____

_____

_____

Before   _____

_____

_____

_____

_____

After

_____

_____

_____

_____

Before _____

_____

_____

_____

_____

After

_____

_____

_____

_____

II. Think about it

❶ How did the objects feel in your hands?

_____

_____

_____

❷ Were some objects easier to squeeze in your hand than other objects? Were some objects harder to squeeze in your hand than other objects?

_____

_____

_____

❸ Create a summary of your observations on the next page. List those objects that were easy to squeeze and those objects that were hard to squeeze.

❹ Put a circle around the objects on which you believe your hand did the most work.

❺ Put a square around the objects on which you believe your hand did the least work.

Easy to
Squeeze

Hard to
Squeeze

_____   _____

_____   _____

_____   _____

_____   _____

_____   _____

_____   _____

_____   _____

_____   _____

III. What did you discover?

❶ For the objects that were easy to squeeze, how much force did you need?

_____

_____

❷ For the objects that were hard to squeeze, how much force did you need?

_____

_____

❸ Did you do more or less work on the objects that were easy to squeeze?

_____

_____

❹ Did you do more or less work on the objects that were hard to squeeze?

_____

_____

❺ Was this result what you expected? Why or why not?

_____

_____

_____

_____

IV. Why?

In this experiment you squeezed several objects between the palm and fingers of your hand. You used your hands like a little force tool. You can do this because your hand has lots of little nerve endings that can detect how soft or hard an object is. You can also tell with your body how easy or hard it is to squeeze an object by noticing your muscles and breath. You can tell with your body if more or less force is needed to change the shape of an object. You can also tell with your body if more or less energy is required to generate the force.

Do you do more work if you use more force and more energy? Not necessarily. You may have noticed that you could easily smash the marshmallow, but it was harder to smash the rubber ball, tennis ball, or rock. Depending on your results, you may have used more force to try to change the shape of the tennis ball or rock, but if they did not actually change shape, you didn't end up doing any work!

V. Just for fun

Using a pair of pliers, squeeze a tennis ball. Observe whether the tennis ball changes shape. Also observe whether it is easier or harder to change the shape of the tennis ball with a pair of pliers than with your hand.

Record your observations.

Tennis Ball

Without Pliers	With Pliers
_____	_____
_____	_____

Experiment 3

Moving Energy in a Toy Car

I. Observe it

❶ Take the board or cardboard sheet, and lay it flat on the ground. Place the toy car on the board or cardboard sheet. Without rolling the toy car, observe what happens.

❷ Write or draw your observations in the space below.

Car flat

❸ Now lift the board or cardboard sheet to the height of your ankles. Again observe what happens. Note whether or not the toy car moves. If it does move, note how it moves in the space below.

❹ Write or draw your observations in the space below.

Car lifted to ankles

❺ Now lift the board or cardboard sheet to the height of your knees. Again observe what happens. Note whether or not the toy car moves. If it does move, note how it moves in the space below.

❻ Write or draw your observations in the space provided below.

Car lifted to knees

_____

_____

_____

_____

_____

_____

_____

_____

_____

❼ Now lift the board or cardboard sheet to the height of your hips. Again observe what happens. Note whether or not the toy car moves. If it does move, note how it moves in the space below.

❽ Write your observations in the space provided below.

Car lifted to hips

❾ Now lift the board or cardboard sheet to the height of your chest. Again observe what happens. Note whether or not the toy car moves. If it does move, note how it moves in the space below.

❿ Write your observations in the space provided below.

Car lifted to chest

_____

_____

_____

_____

_____

_____

_____

_____

_____

Collect your results

In the space below create a table showing your results.

Height of Car	Observations
Car flat	
Car lifted to ankles	
Car lifted to knees	
Car lifted to hips	
Car lifted to chest	

II. Think about it

❶ Think about what the toy car did as you lifted the board higher and higher.

❷ Review what you learned in your student textbook about gravitational stored energy. Recall that gravitational stored energy comes from objects that are elevated above the ground.

❸ Think about both the toy car and gravitational stored energy. Guess which car had the least amount of gravitational stored energy and which car had the greatest amount of gravitational stored energy.

Least _____

Most _____

❹ In the chart on the following page, put a circle around the car that had the least amount of gravitational stored energy.

❺ Put a square around the car that had the greatest amount of gravitational stored energy.

Car flat

Car lifted to ankles

Car lifted to knees

Car lifted to hips

Car lifted to chest

III. What did you discover?

❶ How high did you need to lift the board or cardboard sheet before the car began to move?

_____

_____

❷ Why do you think the car on the ground did not move?

_____

_____

❸ Do you think that as you lifted the board, the car gained more and more gravitational stored energy? Why or why not?

_____

_____

❹ Do you think there was more kinetic energy (moving energy) in the car as you lifted the board? Why or why not?

_____

_____

❺ Was this result what you expected? Why or why not?

_____

_____

IV. Why?

In this experiment you took a toy car and, placing it on a board or cardboard sheet, you observed how the amount of gravitational stored energy changed as you lifted the board. In the first observation, you saw that the car did not move. Sitting flat on the ground, the car did not have any gravitational stored energy since the car was not elevated from the ground. As you lifted the car to your ankles, the car was "given" gravitational stored energy by your body. It may not have moved until you lifted the board to your knees or to your hips, but each time you lifted the car you "gave" the car more gravitational stored energy. Finally, there was enough stored energy for the car to move down the ramp.

When the car moved down the ramp, the gravitational stored energy was converted to kinetic (or moving) energy. You may have observed that the higher you lifted the car, the faster the toy car moved down the ramp. Since the toy car has more gravitational stored energy as it is lifted higher, there is more energy to convert to kinetic energy. As a result, there is more kinetic energy as the car goes down the ramp.

V. Just for fun

How high do you have to lift the toy car to smash a marshmallow at the end of your ramp?

Place a few marshmallows at the end of your ramp. Raise the ramp, and let the toy car roll down. See if you can get the toy car to hit a marshmallow. How high do you have to lift the car to smash the marshmallow? Record your observations.

Height of Car	Did it smash the marshmallow?	
Car flat	YES	NO
Car lifted to ankles	YES	NO
Car lifted to knees	YES	NO
Car lifted to hips	YES	NO
Car lifted to chest	YES	NO

Hint: You may have to lift the ramp to your head or higher! Also, what would happen if you used a heavier car?

Experiment 4

Rolling Marbles

I. Observe it

❶ Take two marbles—one small glass marble and one large glass marble. Roll them both across a smooth surface (wooden floor or table top).

❷ Observe what happens. How far do they go? Do they go straight? How do they stop?

❸ Write or draw a description below of how the marbles rolled. Include any details you think might be important.

Small and large marbles rolling on smooth surface

_____

_____

_____

_____

❹ Take two marbles—one small glass marble and one large glass marble—and roll them across a rough surface (carpeted floor or grass lawn).

❺ Observe what happens. How far do they go? Do they go straight? How do they stop?

❻ Write or draw a description below of how the marbles rolled. Include any details you think might be important.

Small and large marbles rolling on rough surface

_____

_____

_____

_____

II. Think about it

❶ Review what you learned in Chapter 4 of your student textbook about inertia, mass, and friction.

❷ Thinking about the two surfaces (smooth and rough), put a circle around the surface that had the most friction.

Rough surface

Smooth surface

❸ Thinking about the two marbles (large and small) put a square around the size that had the most mass.

Large marble

Small marble

❹ Thinking about the two marbles (large and small), put a triangle around the size that had the most inertia.

Large marble

Small marble

III. What did you discover?

❶ Compare how the small marble moved across the smooth surface with how it moved across the rough surface. Did the marble move differently on different surfaces? Why or why not?

_____

_____

_____

_____

_____

❷ Compare how the large marble moved across the smooth surface with how it moved across the rough surface. Did the marble move differently on different surfaces? Why or why not?

_____

_____

_____

_____

_____

IV. Why?

In this experiment you observed how two marbles of different size (and mass) moved on both a smooth and a rough surface. If you compare your results, you can see how mass and inertia are related and how the force of friction changes how a marble moves. You may have observed that the small marble moves easily on the smooth surface but did not move as easily on a rough surface. You also may have observed that the large marble also moved easily on the smooth surface but not as easily on the rough surface. However, you might also have observed that the larger marble can move further on the rough surface than the smaller marble can.

The larger marble has more mass than the smaller marble. Because it has more mass, it has more inertia. Having more inertia means that it requires more force to start a large marble rolling. But once a large marble is rolling it requires more force to make it stop rolling. The same amount of friction will more easily stop a small marble than a large marble because a small marble has less mass.

In your experiment you observed how the force of friction can stop a moving object. What if you could roll marbles in space? Do you think the marbles would stop? No! The marbles would never stop unless they hit something else. Why? Because once the marbles are rolling, only a force can stop them. In space there is no air, and so there is no force of friction to stop them from moving.

V. Just for fun

What happens if a small marble bumps into a large marble?

Take the large marble and place it in the middle of the table or on the floor. Take the small marble in your fingers and with your thumb shoot the small marble toward the large marble. See if you can hit the large marble with the small marble.

Record your observations.

Try doing the opposite. Place the small marble in the center of the table and hit is with the large marble.

Record your observations on the following page.

Small marble hitting large marble

Large marble hitting small marble

Experiment 5

Lemon Energy

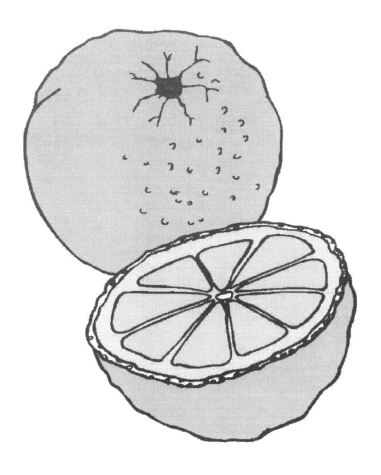

I. Observe it

❶ With the help of an adult, take three lemons and place a copper penny on one end of each lemon and a zinc wire on the other end.

❷ Connect the three lemons together with copper wire. Connect the penny side of one lemon to the zinc side of another lemon.

❸ Take the small LED light and wrap or tape one end of the LED to one of the free wires. Take the other end of the LED and wrap or tape it to the other wire.

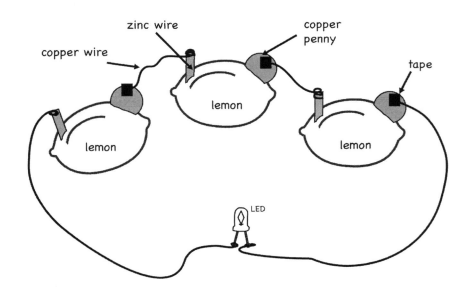

❹ Observe what happens when you attach the LED to the copper wires.

❺ Record your observations below.

_____

_____

_____

_____

❻ Observe what happens to the LED when you disconnect one of the copper wires attached to a penny.

❼ Record your observations below.

_____

_____

_____

_____

❽ Observe what happens to the LED when you disconnect one of the copper wires attached to a zinc wire.

❾ Record your observations below.

Summarize your observations

Trial	What Happened?
All wires connected	
Penny wire disconnected	
Zinc wire disconnected	

II. Think about it

❶ Think about how you set the lemon batteries up. Think about how you connected the wires and how you connected the LED to the lemons.

❷ Review what you learned in your student text about chemical energy and batteries.

❸ Circle the statement that is true based on your observations.

The LED will light only when all the wires are connected.

The LED will light with the penny wire disconnected.

The LED will light when the zinc wire is disconnected.

❹ Think about any problems you might have had with your experiment. List them below.

_____

_____

_____

_____

_____

III. What did you discover?

❶ Were you able to get the LED to light up? Why or why not?

_____

_____

_____

_____

_____

❷ Did the LED light up when one or more of the wires was disconnected? Why or why not?

_____

_____

_____

_____

_____

_____

_____

_____

IV. Why?

I bet you didn't know a lemon could be a battery! We normally don't think of lemons as batteries, but as food. However, in this experiment you assembled an electric circuit using lemons as batteries. The lemons contain acid. The acid in the lemons reacts with the copper and zinc metals, and this creates a chemical reaction. This chemical reaction inside the lemons produces electricity that can be used to power a small LED. [The term LED stands for "Light Emitting Diode" which is like a little light bulb that does not require lots of electricity to run].

Three lemons are used to light the LED. One lemon would not have generated enough electricity to run the LED, so three lemons are needed. The lemons were connected to each other in such a way that the electricity of all the lemons could be added together. When all three lemons are working together, there is enough electricity generated by the chemical reaction to light up the LED.

When disconnecting one or more of the wires, the LED stopped working. By disconnecting the wires, the battery energy in each lemon can no longer be added to that of the other lemons and the electricity cannot flow to the LED and the LED stops working. The lemons are a form of stored chemical energy, and once they are connected to each other in the right way, they can generate enough electricity to power a small LED.

V. Just for fun

Disconnect one of the wires from the LED. With your fingers on one hand, hold the wire connected to the lemons. With your fingers on the other hand, hold the metal end from the disconnected LED.

What happens?

Experiment 6

Sticky Balloons

I. Observe it

❶ Take a rubber balloon and blow it up with air. Close the end. Place it on a wall. Observe whether it sticks to the wall.

❷ Rub the balloon in your hair without popping it.

❸ Carefully pull the balloon away from your hair and observe whether your hair sticks to the balloon. If your hair sticks to the balloon, continue to step ❹ but if your hair does not stick to the balloon, rub the balloon another time in your hair.

❹ Test how sticky the balloon is by placing it on a wall. Observe whether the balloon sticks or falls off the wall.

❺ Record your observations in the space provided on the next page. Use the following questions.

   ① Does the balloon stick?
   ② How long does the balloon stick? 1 second? 2 seconds? 10 seconds? Longer than a minute?
   ③ Does the balloon move around or stay still?
   ④ What happens if you blow gently on the balloon? Does it stay stuck or does it fall off?

❻ Repeat steps ❷-❺ using several materials such as wool or cotton clothing, metal or wood surfaces.

Hair

_____

_____

_____

_____

_____

_____

_____

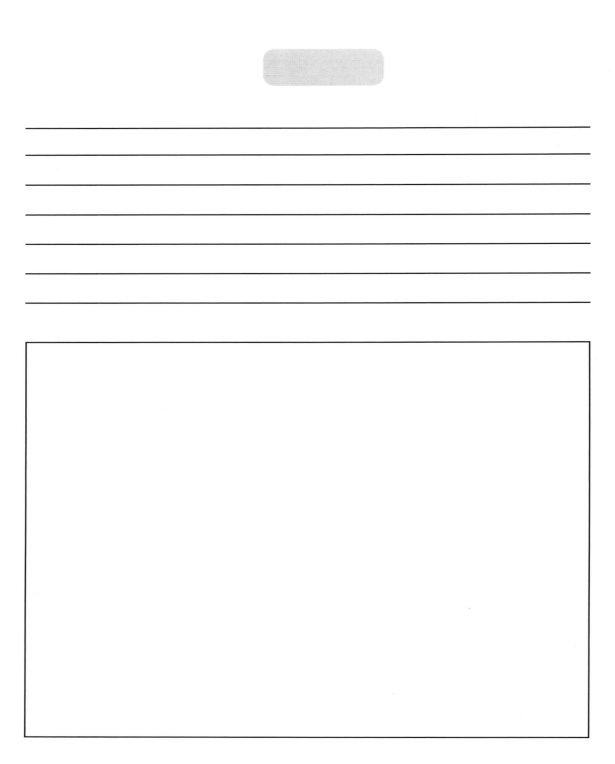

II. Think about it

❶ Think about the balloon and the different materials you used to charge the balloon.

❷ Review what you learned in your student text about electrons, charges, and force.

❸ Create a chart on the following page that lists the materials or surfaces you used in your experiment. Organize the list to begin with those materials or surfaces that created the most charge and to end with those that created the least charge.

Most Charge	
Least Charge	

III. What did you discover?

❶ Were you able to get the balloon to carry a charge? Why or why not?

_____

_____

_____

_____

_____

❷ Did some materials charge the balloon more than other materials or were they all the same?

_____

_____

_____

_____

_____

❸ Could you tell how much charge the balloon gained by attaching it to the wall? Why or why not?

_____

_____

_____

_____

_____

IV. Why?

In this experiment you explored how a balloon can pick up electrons from other objects. When a balloon picks up electrons from another object, the balloon becomes charged. The very first time you placed the balloon on the wall, before you rubbed it in your hair, the balloon likely fell off. Why? It fell off because the balloon did not carry any additional charges.

When you rubbed the balloon in your hair, the balloon picked up electrons from your hair. The electrons are negatively charged, so the balloon became negatively charged. A negatively charged balloon will stick to surfaces that are slightly positively charged. If the balloon stuck to the wall, then the wall was slightly positively charged.

You could test how many electrons the balloon picked up by observing how easily the balloon would stick to a wall after it was charged. If the balloon stuck a lot, then there were lots of electrons. If the balloon only stuck a little, then there were fewer electrons.

It is possible that it was difficult to get the balloon to become charged no matter what material or surface was used. If you discovered this, that's Ok. Check the humidity in your area. If it was humid when you did the experiment, the electrons could not stay very long on the balloon.

V. Just for fun

Take two balloons and tie a piece of string to the end of each balloon. Tie the other ends of the strings together, and hang the balloons from a doorway or shower rod. What happens?

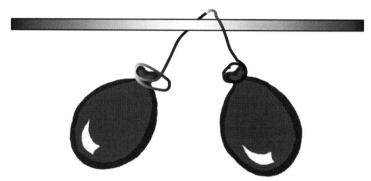

Take the balloons and rub them both in your hair. Let the balloons go and allow them to float back together. What happens?

Record your observations below.

Before rubbing	After rubbing

Experiment 7

Moving Electrons

I. Observe it

❶ With the help of an adult, set up the lemon battery from Chapter 5. Make sure the LED is illuminated.

❷ With the help of an adult, take one of the wires and cut it in half. Observe what happens to the LED. Write or draw your observations below.

Wires apart

_____

_____

_____

❸ Strip the plastic from the ends of the wire that was cut in half. Reconnect the two loose wires by twisting the metal ends together. Observe what happens to the LED. Write or draw your observations below.

Wires connected

_____

_____

_____

❹ Disconnect the wires and place a piece of styrofoam between the wires. Observe what happens to the LED. Write or draw your observations below.

Styrofoam

_____

_____

_____

❺ Remove the styrofoam from between the wires. Reconnect the wires by twisting them together. Observe what happens to the LED. Write or draw your observations below.

Wires connected

_____

_____

_____

❻ Repeat steps ❹-❺ using the different materials listed in the Teacher's Manual. Test all of the materials listed. Record your observations in the space provided.

Plastic Block

Cotton Ball

_____

_____

_____

_____

_____

_____

_____

Nickel Coin

_____

_____

_____

_____

_____

_____

_____

Metal Paper Clip

_____

_____

_____

_____

_____

_____

_____

Plastic Paper Clip

_____
_____
_____
_____
_____
_____
_____

❼ Summarize your results below. Write "ON" or "OFF" in the LED column for each of the items listed:

Item	LED
Start – wires connected	
wires apart	
wires connected	
styrofoam	
plastic block	
cotton ball	
nickel coin	
metal paper clip	
plastic paper clip	

II. Think about it

❶ Think about the LED and the different materials you used between the wires.

❷ Review what you learned in your student textbook about moving electric charges.

❸ Use the chart below to organize the materials you tested. Place those items that illuminated the LED in one column and those items that did not illuminate the LED in the other column.

LED "ON"	LED "OFF"

III. What did you discover?

❶ Which items illuminated the LED?

_____

_____

_____

❷ Which items did not illuminate the LED?

_____

_____

_____

_____

❸ Were the items that illuminated the LED metals?

_____

❹ Were the items that did not illuminate the LED non-metals?

_____

_____

❺ Why do you think metals illuminated the LED and non-metals did not?

_____

_____

_____

_____

_____

IV. Why?

In this experiment you explored how electrons moved (or didn't move) through different materials. When the lemon batteries are connected with metal wires, the electrons can flow freely through the wires and light up the LED. When the metal wire was cut, the electrons were stopped from flowing through to the LED. When the metal wires were reconnected, the electrons flowed through again to light up the LED.

You discovered that some materials will allow electrons to flow through them and some materials won't. Electrons easily flow through most metals. Metals, and any other materials that allows electrons to flow through them, are called conductors. Electrons do not flow through most plastics (styrofoam, plastic blocks, or plastic paper clips), cotton balls, and other similar materials. These materials are called insulators.

There are also materials that are reluctant to allow electrons to flow through them. These materials are called resistors. Resistors will allow a few electrons to flow through them, but not all electrons. Resistors are actually used in electronic circuits to control the amount of electron flow.

V. Just for fun

Take the two ends of the wire that were cut. Place both ends in a glass of water. Observe what happens to the LED.

Now add a tablespoon of salt to the water. Stir the salt until it has completely dissolved. Observe what happens to the LED.

Record your observations below.

Wire ends in water

Wire ends in salt water

Experiment 8

Magnet Poles

I. Observe it

❶ Take the two magnets and place them on a table several inches apart with each "N" facing each other

❷ Gently push one "N" closer to the other "N." Observe what happens. Write or draw your observations below.

Trial 1

_____

_____

_____

❸ Place the two magnets on the table several inches apart. Reverse the direction of one of the magnets so that the "N" is facing the "S."

❹ Gently push the "N" closer to the "S." Observe what happens. Write or draw your observations below.

Trial 2

_____

_____

_____

❺ Repeat steps ❶-❹ several times. See how close you can bring the two magnets together before something changes.

Write or draw your observations in the spaces provided.

Trial 3

_____

_____

_____

Trial 4

Trial 5

Trial 6

Trial 7

Trial 8

Trial 9

Trial 10

❻ Summarize your results in the chart.

* ♦ Mark the trials N–N or N–S.

* ♦ Mark the trials where the magnets came together

* ♦ Mark the trials where the magnets pushed apart.

Trial	N–N or S–S	"Together" or "Apart"
Trial 1		
Trial 2		
Trial 3		
Trial 4		
Trial 5		
Trial 6		
Trial 7		
Trial 8		
Trial 9		
Trial 10		

II. Think about it

❶ Think about the magnets and the different ways you pushed the magnets together.

❷ Review what you learned in your student textbook about magnets and magnetic poles.

❸ Look at the results you gathered in the previous section. Cover up the second column of the table and look only at the third column. Without looking at the second column, write down those trials where the poles were the "same" and those trials where the poles were "opposite."

Trial	"Same" or "Opposite"
Trial 1	
Trial 2	
Trial 3	
Trial 4	
Trial 5	
Trial 6	
Trial 7	
Trial 8	
Trial 9	
Trial 10	

❹ Uncover the second column from the previous page. Do your answers match the second column of the previous table?

III. What did you discover?

❶ What happened when you pushed the two "N" ends of the magnets together?

_____

_____

_____

_____

❷ What happened when you reversed one of the magnets and pushed them together again?

_____

_____

_____

_____

❸ If you had two magnets where the poles were not labeled "N" and "S," could you guess which poles were the same and which were opposite? Why or why not?

_____

_____

_____

_____

_____

_____

IV. Why?

In this experiment you explored magnetic poles. Magnets have two poles called "North" and "South." When two opposite poles (North and South) come together, they attract each other and the magnets will snap together. When two of the same pole (North and North, or South and South) come together, they repel each other and the magnets will move away from each other.

Even though you may not know which pole is "North" and which pole is "South" by "playing" with the magnets (by reversing one of the magnets on the table and then switching it back), you could explore how different poles react to each other. Reversing the magnet several times gave you information about when the magnets were coming together and when they were moving apart. As you observed the magnets coming together or moving apart, you observed the different poles.

Scientists have to "play" with things around them to figure out what is happening. Scientists do different "trials," just like you did, to find out what happens when some part of an experiment is changed. By "playing" with their experiments, scientists make observations they might have missed if they did the experiment only one way.

V. Just for fun

Take a magnet and find out which surfaces in your house the magnet will attract or not attract.

Record your observations below.

Surface	"Attract" or "Not Attract"

Experiment 9

Splitting Light

I. Observe it

❶ Using one prism, go outside on a sunny day and hold the prism in the sunlight.

❷ Rotate the prism until you can see different colors.

❸ Draw what you see in the space provided.

❹ Using colored pencils or crayons, color the various bands of light you see coming from the prism. Pay special attention to how the bands of colored light are arranged.

Sunlight

❺ Using a flashlight, shine light through one of the flat edges of the prism. Try to find a clear wall to project the light onto so you can observe the reflected light.

❻ Again, rotate the prism and observe any colors that might show on the wall.

❼ Draw your observations in the space provided.

Flashlight

❽ Repeat steps ❶-❹ using two prisms. Shine sunlight through two prisms at the same time holding both prisms side by side. Adjust the angle of each until you see light going through both prisms.

❾ Draw your observations below.

Sunlight
Two prisms

⑩ Repeat steps ❶-❹ using two prisms and a flashlight. Shine the flashlight through the two prisms at the same time holding both prisms side by side. Adjust the angle of each until you see light going through both prisms.

Flashlight
Two prisms

II. Think about it

❶ Think about how both the sunlight and the light from the flashlight went through the prisms.

❷ Review what you learned about waves and light in Chapter 9 of the student textbook. Think about how "white" light is a mixture of different light waves.

❸ Look carefully at the drawings you created for a single prism in the sunlight. Knowing that red light is a slow, long wavelength of light and that blue light is a fast, short wavelength of light, can you guess which wavelengths are shorter and which are longer? (Hint, the longer wavelengths will be closer to red than blue and the shorter wavelengths will be closer to blue than red on your drawing.)

Light	Shorter or Longer than	Light
green		orange
blue		yellow
orange		blue
red		yellow
violet		green
yellow		red

III. What did you discover?

❶ What happened when you held a single prism outside in the sunlight?

_____

_____

_____

❷ What happened when you used a flashlight to shine light through a single prism?

_____

_____

_____

❸ What happened when you took two prisms outside in the sunlight or used a flashlight with two prisms?

_____

_____

_____

_____

_____

_____

_____

_____

IV. Why?

In this experiment you explored how white light is really a mixture of different colored light. You discovered that the different colors can be separated from each other using a prism. Once the different colors separated you were able to observe all of the different colors of the rainbow.

A prism takes "white light," which is a mixture of colored light wavelengths, and bends each wavelength of light. Because the wavelengths of light are all different, when they bend, they come out of the prism separated from each other. Once they are separated from each other, you can see the individual colors. Raindrops work the same way a prism does, and when it rains you can often see a rainbow of colors. The rainbow is generated by the raindrops bending the sunlight and splitting the different colors.

When you used two prisms, side by side, you should have observed an "inverted" rainbow. That is the colors from the double prism are opposite the colors from the single prism. This happens because the second prism bends the colors a second time and flips them around. However, because the colors are already separated, they don't separate further. With two prisms you don't see a different rainbow than you saw from a single prism, but you see an inverted rainbow.

V. Just for fun

Test different types of light sources. You have already
used a flashlight and sunlight. What happens if you use a
mercury bulb or a fluorescent bulb. What happens if you
use a colored light bulb?

Record your observations below.

Light source	Observations

Experiment 10

Playing with Physics

I. Observe it

❶ Take two marbles. Roll one marble into the other marble.

❷ Draw what happens to the two marbles.

Two marbles

❸ Take three playing cards and make a small card house.

❹ Roll a marble so it hits the card house. Draw what happens to the cards.

Marble hits card house

❺ Find a shallow jar top. A pickle jar top would work well. Fill it with vinegar.

❻ Add a tablespoon of baking soda to the vinegar.

❼ Draw what happens.

Vinegar and Baking Soda

❽ Place the card house above the shallow lid filled with vinegar.

❾ Place a tablespoon of baking soda on top of the card house. Tip the card house with your finger so the baking soda falls into the vinegar. Record your observations below.

Card house
plus baking
soda and vinegar

⑩ Now assemble all the steps into a short series. Take one marble and place it a few inches from the card house. Place the shallow lid of vinegar under the card house. Place a tablespoon of baking soda on the card house. Roll the second marble into the marble close to the card house. Record your observations below.

Marble-->Marble-->Card House w/baking soda-->Vinegar

II. Think about it

❶ Think about the different types of energy you assembled in this short series.

❷ Review what you learned about energy in Chapter 10. Note how energy is neither created nor destroyed, but simply converted from one form to another.

❸ In the table below list the type of energy you think the object started with and the type of energy you think it was converted to. Use the following energy descriptions:

Kinetic energy (rolling)
Kinetic energy (falling)
Potential energy (chemical)
Potential energy (gravitational)
Chemical energy

Object	Started With	Converted To
marble-->marble		
marble-->card house		
card house upright--> card house falling		
baking soda or vinegar -->baking soda + vinegar		

III. What did you discover?

❶ What happened to the energy of one marble when you rolled it into another marble that was not moving?

_____

_____

❷ What happened to the energy of the marble when you rolled it to hit the card house?

_____

_____

❸ What happened to the energy in the baking soda (or the vinegar) when you added the two together?

_____

_____

❹ What happened to the energy of the marble you rolled when you put all the steps together?

_____

_____

❺ What do you think happened to all the energy at the end of your experiment? Where did it go?

_____

_____

IV. Why?

In this experiment you explored how different forms of energy can be converted from one form to another. You rolled a marble and watched the marble use kinetic energy to move. You had that marble strike another marble and observed how the kinetic energy of the first marble was converted into kinetic energy in the second marble.

You also rolled a marble to hit a card house, converting the kinetic energy of the rolling marble into the kinetic energy of the falling cards. You also observed how the gravitational potential energy of the top card was converved into kinetic energy when it fell.

When you put the vinegar underneath the card house, and placed baking soda on top, you converted chemical potential energy into chemical energy when the baking soda and vinegar came together.

In each case, you observed energy being converted from one form into another. This is how energy works. You can't create energy and you can't destroy it. You can only move it from one object to another or convert it from one form to another.

What do you think happened to all the energy at the end of your experiment? Where did it go?

V. Just for fun

Create your own series for converting energy from one form to another.

Here are some ideas—see if you can connect them.

- ❖ Rolling marbles
- ❖ Dominoes side by side
- ❖ Vinegar and baking soda
- ❖ Stacked blocks
- ❖ An electric car
- ❖ An electric train
- ❖ Marshmallow on one end of a tongue depressor, a steel ball or marble dropped on the other end

Made in the USA
Charleston, SC
05 March 2010